TERMITES
Mound Builders

Lynn George

PowerKiDS
press.
New York

Published in 2011 by The Rosen Publishing Group, Inc.
29 East 21st Street, New York, NY 10010

First Edition

Editor: Joanne Randolph
Book Design: Kate Laczynski
Photo Researcher: Greg Tucker

Photo Credits: Cover, p. 1 John W. Banagan/Getty Images; cover (inset), p. 15 George Grall/Getty Images; back cover and interior blueprint © www.istockphoto.com/Branko Miokovic; pp. 4, 5, 6, 7, 10–11, 14 (right), 16, 17, 18 (termite) Shutterstock.com; p. 8 © George Lepp/age fotostock.com; pp. 9, 22 Mona Lisa Productions/Getty Images; pp. 12–13 © Biosphoto/Vincent Jean-Christophe/Peter Arnold, Inc.; p. 14 (left) Tier Und Naturfotografie J. & C. Sohns/Getty Images; p. 18 (hard hat) © www.iStockphoto.com/Don Nichols; pp. 18–19 © S. Sailer/A. Sailer/age fotostock.com; p. 19 Kim Taylor/Getty Images; p. 20 © www.iStockphoto.com/Melinda Fawver; p. 21 © www.iStockphoto.com/Ross Lewis.

Library of Congress Cataloging-in-Publication Data

George, Lynn.
  Termites : mound builders / Lynn George. — 1st ed.
     p. cm. — (Animal architects)
  Includes index.
  ISBN 978-1-4488-0696-6 (library binding) — ISBN 978-1-4488-1353-7 (pbk.) —
ISBN 978-1-4488-1354-4 (6-pack)
  1. Termites—Habitations—Juvenile literature. I. Title.
  QL529.G46 2011
  595.7'36—dc22
                                   2010008872

Manufactured in the United States of America

CPSIA Compliance Information: Batch #WS10PK: For Further Information contact Rosen Publishing, New York, New York at 1-800-237-9932

CONTENTS

TINY TERMITES

Have you heard of termites? They are small bugs that look somewhat like pale ants. They live in large colonies, as do ants. However, they are not ants. Look closely, and you will see how termites differ from ants. Ants have thin parts between their two back body parts that are like waists.

Termites may look a bit like ants, but they are more closely related to cockroaches. Termites have strong mouthparts to help them chew wood and other matter.

Many of us picture huge mounds like this one when we think of termites. Not all termites build mounds, though.

Termites do not. Termites are generally white, while ants are dark in color.

Many people consider termites pests because some kinds eat wood and crops. Yet most are **beneficial**.

Termites have special talents. They eat food few animals can eat. They break down dead plant matter and return **nutrients** to the soil. They are also natural **architects**. Some termites build large nests. Other kinds build wonderful, huge mounds that are taller than houses!

5

SO MANY TERMITES!

Would you believe there are about 2,750 species, or kinds, of termites? Of all of these termites, only about 275 termite species are pests.

Unlike most bugs, termites lack thick coverings to **protect** their bodies. They have to stay hidden from the Sun and from their many enemies,

A termite with wings is called an alate. Alates break off their wings once they are ready to start a new colony.

such as birds, ants, frogs, and other animals. Termites do not leave their homes often.

Scientists group termites based on where they make their homes. There are two main groups.

One group lives in wood. The other group makes tunnels and nests in soil. The second group includes the termites that build giant mounds.

WHAT IS FOR DINNER?

What have you eaten today? Maybe you had fruit, cheese, bread, and some meat. People eat food to get nutrients that keep our bodies healthy. Termites need healthy foods, too. However, termites do not eat the same things people eat. If you were a worker termite, you would have eaten wood, grass, leaves, **humus**, or even cardboard. You might have eaten **fungus**, too.

Drywood termites, such as these, like to eat wood and are generally the ones found in houses.

Termites get stiff matter called cellulose and lignin from their food. This matter is very hard to **digest.** Few animals can get nutrients from

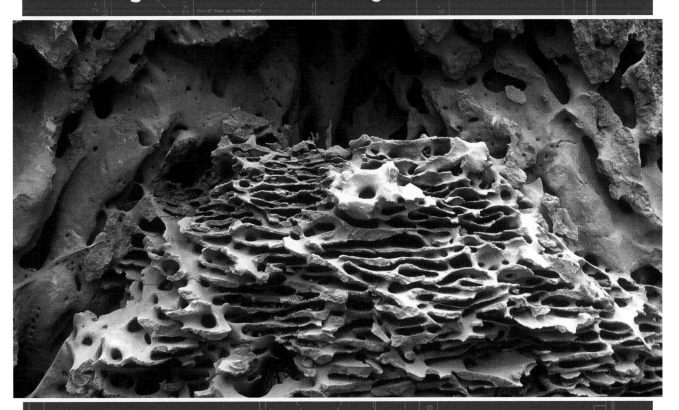

them. Even termites need help. Most termites have tiny creatures in their guts that help them digest cellulose and lignin. Some get help from the fungus they eat!

EVERY TERMITE HAS A JOB

Just as people live in towns and cities, termites live in colonies. However, not everyone in your town is related to everyone else. In a termite colony, everyone belongs to one huge family!

A colony has three major **castes**. Each caste does certain jobs. Most termites are workers. They build and care for the nest. They gather food and water. They

The large white shape here is a termite queen. Her only job is to lay eggs. All the smaller termites around her are workers that bring her food and bring eggs to cells.

care for the young. Soldiers form another caste. They protect the colony. Workers and soldiers are blind and wingless.

Termites in the third caste are reproductives. They get their name because they can produce young. The main reproductives are the king and queen who founded the colony. Others will leave to found new colonies.

A TERMITE'S LIFE

Termites begin as eggs. The queen lays the eggs. Workers care for the eggs and the young that **hatch** from them. The young are called nymphs. They molt, or shed their skin, several times as they grow.

Most animals reach adulthood when the body grows and develops enough to make babies of its own. For most termites, though, something surprising

happens. The nymphs that become workers and soldiers stop growing. They never become fully developed adults.

Only the few nymphs that become reproductives continue to grow and develop. Once they are adults, they leave the colony, lay their own eggs, and begin new colonies.

WHY TERMITES NEED NESTS

This termite nest has been built on the side of a tree.

Termites build tunnels like this one to keep themselves safe as they try to reach wood that is not touching the ground.

You may think that most animals and bugs spend time outside every day. Termites cannot do that. Because of their thin skin, the Sun and dry air can easily hurt or kill them. Therefore, termites build warm, wet, dark nests to protect themselves.

Termites spend most of their lives inside their nests. Workers may go outside at night to feed.

Different termite types build different kinds of nests. Some termites build nests in wood. Some build nests high in trees. Others build nests in soil. All of these different nests are well planned. They have many tunnels and rooms. They are even built in such a way as to make sure the nest does not get too hot or too cold!

MONSTER MOUNDS

Like people's homes, termite mounds come in many shapes and sizes. There are rounded mounds. There are pointed **cathedral** mounds. There are thin, flat magnetic, or **compass**, mounds that point north and south.

Compass mounds may be 13 feet (4 m) tall. That is as high as one tall person standing one on top of

The termite mound on the left is in Nepal, and the one on the right is in Australia. Worker termites built both mounds using mud, waste, and saliva.

another! Cathedral mounds can be 30 feet (9 m) tall. That is as tall as a three-story building!

Inside the mounds are cells, or rooms, joined by tunnels. There are also tunnels to let air in and out. Tunnels below the mounds may go deep into the ground.

INSIDE VIEW:
Termite Mounds

1

Let's take a look at larger termite mounds, such as cathedral and magnetic mounds. The outside of these mounds is hard. Animals may sit on these mounds to look for danger or food. Some birds and lizards even build nests on these mounds.

Termites also dig special chimneys in their mounds. Hot air rises through the mound through special tunnels. It leaves the mound through the chimneys, which open to the outside.

8

Holes in the base of the mound lead into the cellar. Cool, fresh air enters the mound through these holes.

7

Termites dig tunnels below the mound, too. These tunnels may go down 200 feet (61 m) into the ground to find water. Other animals sometimes make homes in the tunnels.

6

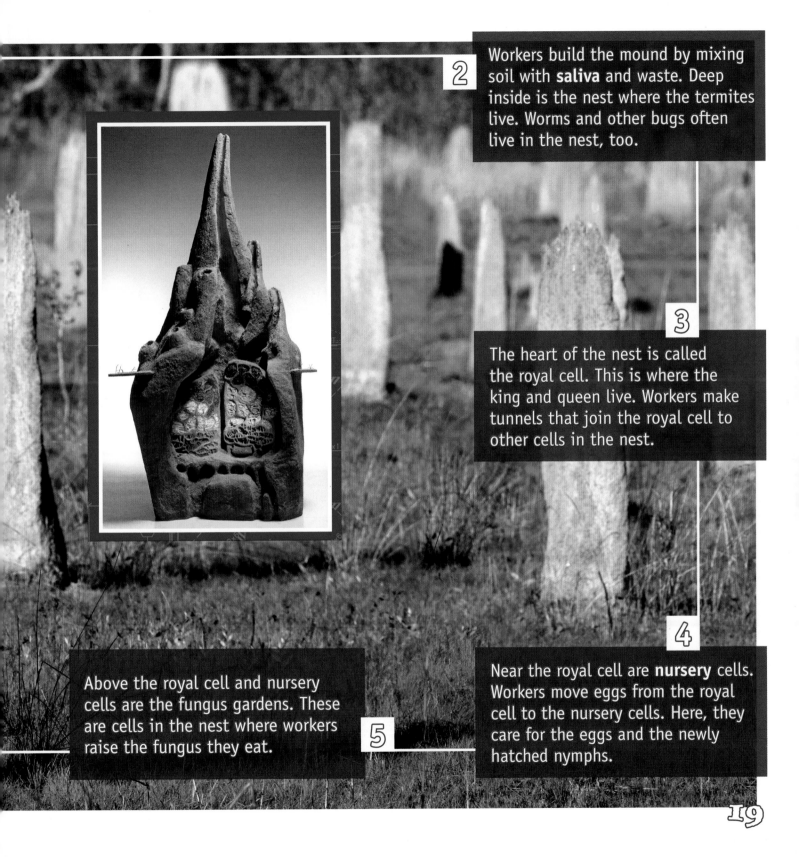

2 Workers build the mound by mixing soil with **saliva** and waste. Deep inside is the nest where the termites live. Worms and other bugs often live in the nest, too.

3 The heart of the nest is called the royal cell. This is where the king and queen live. Workers make tunnels that join the royal cell to other cells in the nest.

4 Near the royal cell are **nursery** cells. Workers move eggs from the royal cell to the nursery cells. Here, they care for the eggs and the newly hatched nymphs.

5 Above the royal cell and nursery cells are the fungus gardens. These are cells in the nest where workers raise the fungus they eat.

STARTING A NEW NEST

How do tiny termites build huge mounds? It takes a long time. A mound starts with a king and queen that have left their home colonies. They dig a small cell in the ground. The queen starts laying eggs. The king and queen care for the eggs and young at first. When there are enough workers, they take over these jobs. The workers also begin to build a larger mound or nest. They need to make more room for all the new termites that will be born.

It may take 2 years for the mound to appear above the ground. It grows less than 1 inch (2.5 cm) each year. The biggest mounds may be 70 or even 100 years old!

ARE TERMITES PESTS?

You may have heard people say that termites are pests. It is true that some types hurt homes and eat crops. However ninety percent, or 9 out of 10, of them are beneficial.

Termites' waste makes the soil better. Their tunnels let air and water go deeper into soil. Better soil means more kinds of plants and animals.

In Africa, people cook termites and eat them. They are even used in medicine in some places. Scientists have also found that termites make hydrogen when they eat certain foods. This information may help scientists make cleaner kinds of energy. Do termites sound like pests to you?

GLOSSARY

architects (AHR-kuh-tekts) People who have ideas and make plans for buildings.

beneficial (beh-nuh-FIH-shul) Helpful or good.

castes (KASTS) Levels or groups of insects in a colony.

cathedral (kuh-THEE-drul) A large church that is run by a bishop or something that looks like one.

compass (KUM-pus) A tool made up of a freely turning magnetic needle that tells which direction is north or something that points north like a compass.

digest (dy-JEST) To break down food so that the body can use it.

fungus (FUN-gis) A living thing that is like a plant but that does not have leaves, flowers, or green color and that does not make its own food.

hatch (HACH) To come out of an egg.

humus (HUH-mis) Dark brown matter formed from the remains of dead plants and animals.

nursery (NURS-ree) A place where babies are cared for.

nutrients (NOO-tree-ents) Food that a living thing needs to live and grow.

protect (pruh-TEKT) To keep from being hurt or to keep safe.

saliva (suh-LY-vuh) The liquid in the mouth that starts to break down food and helps food move down the throat.

INDEX

WEB SITES

Due to the changing nature of Internet links, PowerKids Press has developed an online list of Web sites related to the subject of this book. This site is updated regularly. Please use this link to access the list:

www.powerkidslinks.com/arch/termite/